TALKABOUT

Sand

TALKABOUT
Sand

Text: Angela Webb
Photography: Chris Fairclough

Franklin Watts
London/New York/Sydney/Toronto

©1986 Franklin Watts
First published in Great Britain by

Franklin Watts
12a Golden Square
London W1

First published in the USA by

Franklin Watts Inc
387 Park Avenue South
New York 10016

ISBN: UK edition 0 86313 478 5
ISBN: US edition 0–531–10370–6
Library of Congress
Catalog Card No: 87–50233

Editor: Ruth Thomson
Design: Edward Kinsey
Additional Photographs: Zefa

Typesetting: Keyspools Ltd
Printed in Italy

About this book

This book has been written for young children – in the playgroup, school and at home.

Its aim is to increase children's awareness of the world around them and to promote thought and discussion about topics of scientific interest.

The book draws on examples from a child's own environment. The activities and experiments suggested are simple enough for children to conduct themselves, with only a little help from an adult, using objects and materials which will be familiar to them.

Children will gain most from the book if the book is used together with practical activities. Such experiences will help to consolidate knowledge and also suggest new ideas for further exploration and experimentation.

The themes explored in this book include:

Sand comes from rocks and shells.
Sand is made up of single grains.
Dry sand 'flows' like a liquid.
Sand absorbs water.
Sand behaves differently when wet.

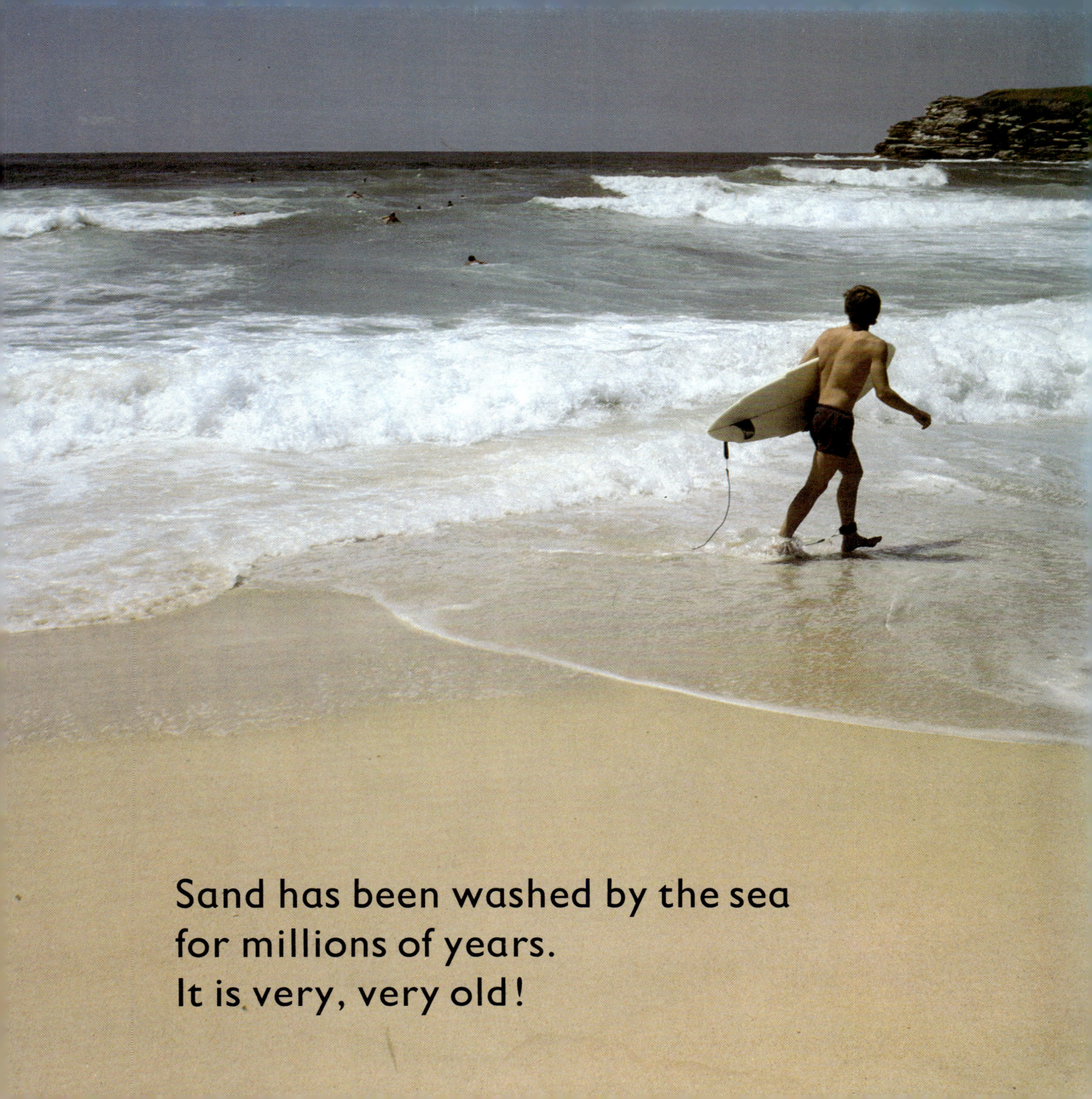

Sand has been washed by the sea
for millions of years.
It is very, very old!

Where does sand come from?

The sea knocks
rocks and shells together.
They break into small pieces.

Deserts were once covered by the sea but the water dried up long ago.

Sand is made up
of tiny pieces of rock and shell.
These are called grains.

Look at these three kinds of sand.

What differences can you see?
Are all the grains the same size?

Run some sand through your fingers.
How does it feel?

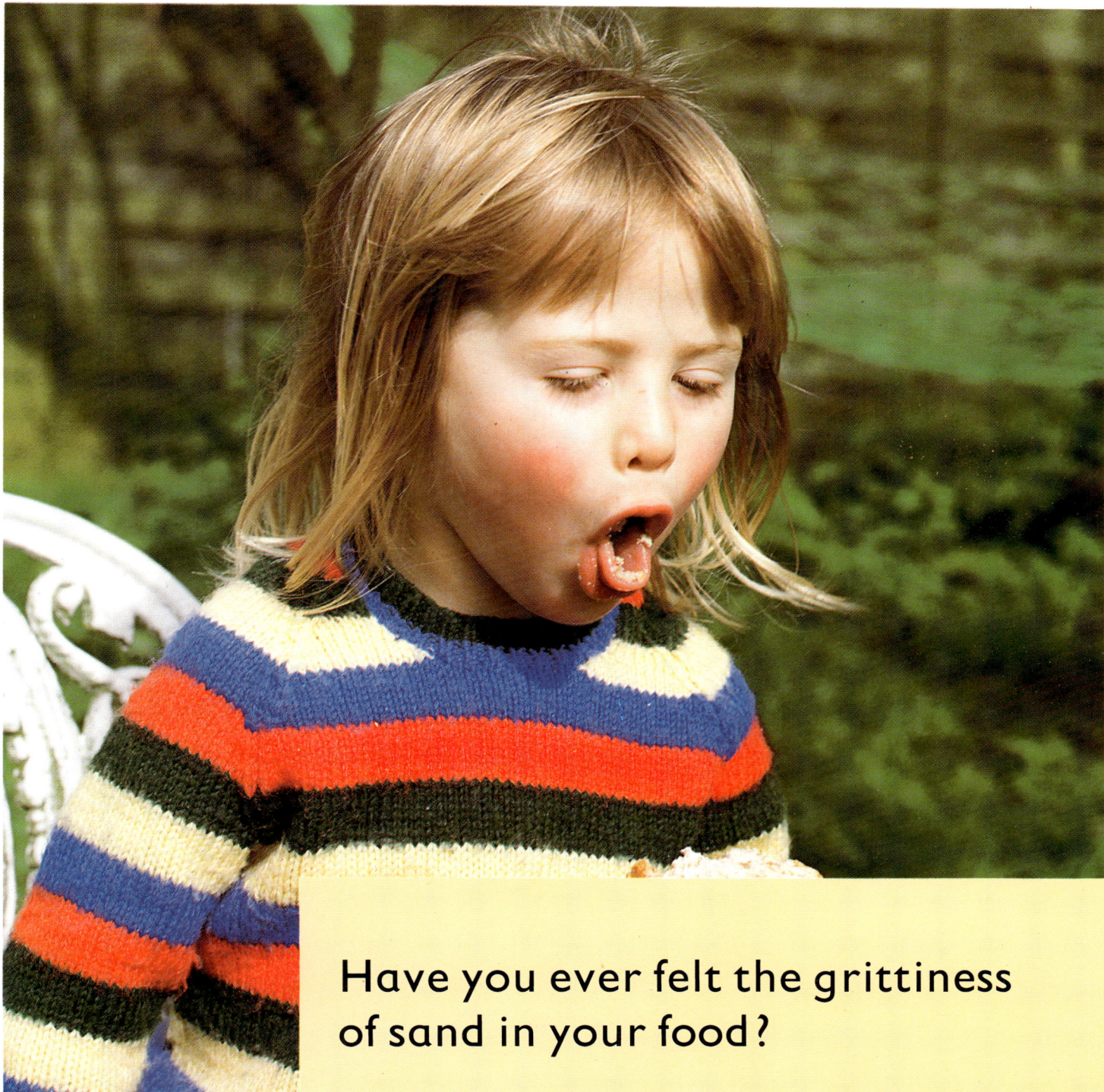

Have you ever felt the grittiness of sand in your food?

Because sand is made of grains,
it can move.
Stir some fine, dry sand
with a spoon.

What happens?

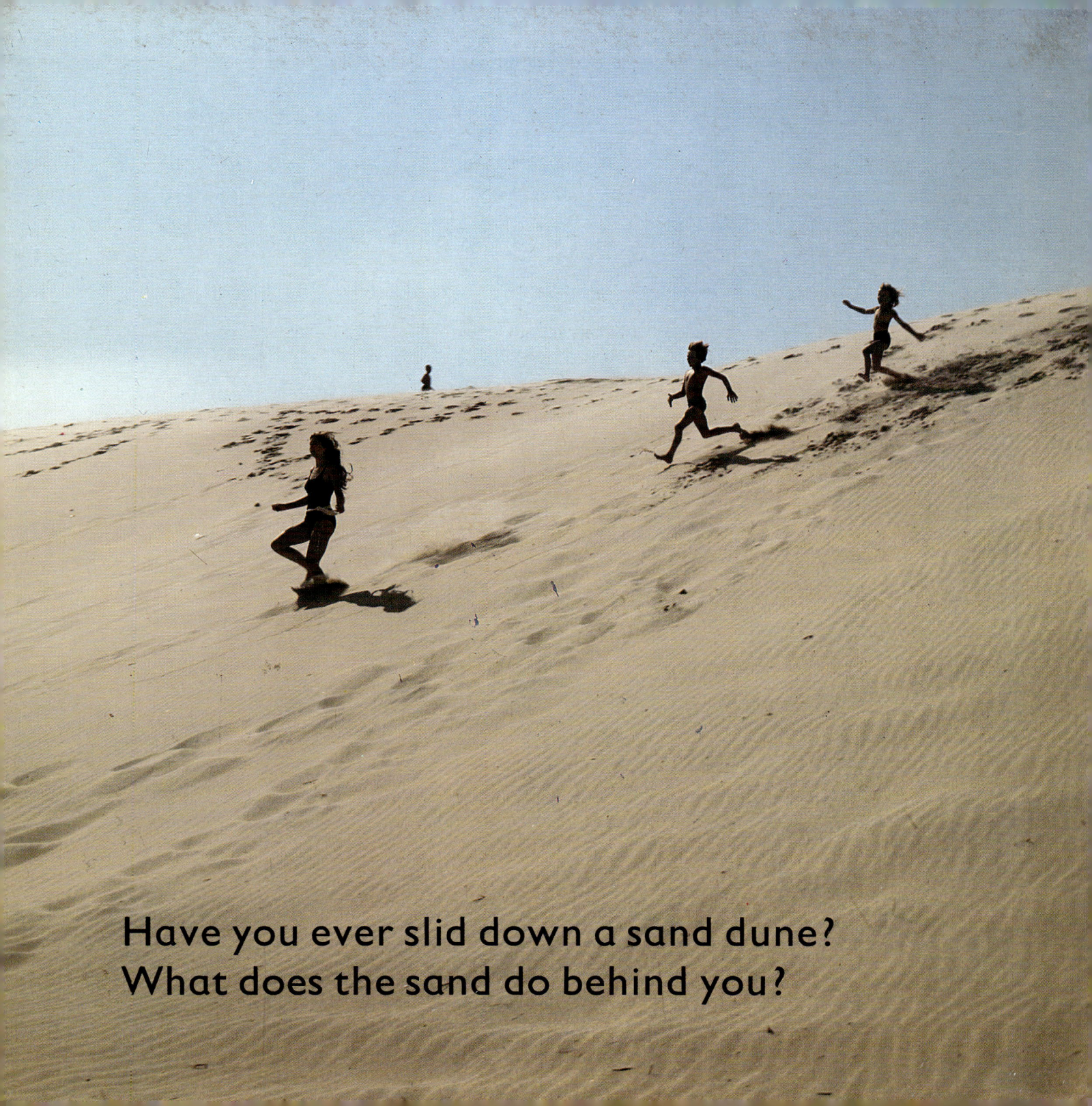

Have you ever slid down a sand dune?
What does the sand do behind you?

Watch how grains move if you blow them.

When wind blows sand,
what patterns can you see?

Watch sand run down a chute.
What shape is it making in the bowl?

Watch sand run through an egg timer.

Which timer will finish first? Why?
Which timer will finish last? Why?

Make a timer.
Hold a funnel
over an empty pot.
Pour all the sand
from a full pot
into it.

You can make
pictures with sand.

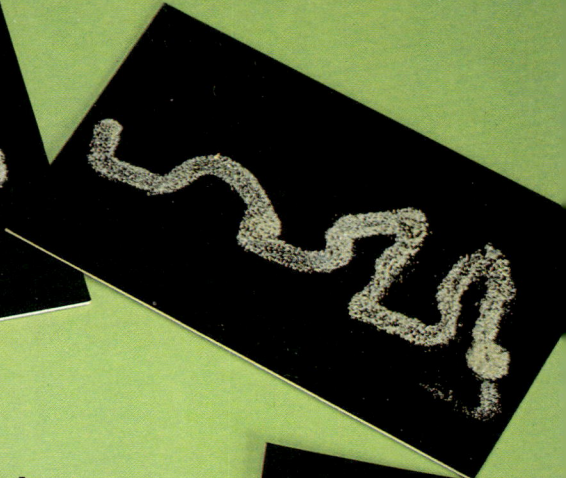

Pour water
on to some dry sand.

What happens?

Water makes the grains stick together.

If you drop some damp sand
does it fall grain by grain,
like dry sand?

It falls in lumps.

How else is damp sand different
from dry sand?
Feel it with your hands . . .

and your feet.

Which is
better for
making shapes?

Wet sand like this . . .

or dry sand like this?

What kind of sand is best
for drawing in . . .

printing patterns . . .

building castles . . .

or making tunnels?

Wet or dry, sand is fun!